The Gift *of* Teaching

Carol Kelly-Gangi

Jude Patterson

BARNES
&NOBLE
BOOKS
NEW YORK

The Gift of Teaching

A Book of Favorite Quotations

to Inspire and Encourage

2002 Barnes & Noble Books

ISBN 0-7607-3319-8

Book design by Nicola Ferguson

Printed and bound in the United States of America

02 03 04 05 PCC 9 8 7 6 5 4 3

To John, John Christopher, Brian, and

Kaitlin with love.

Teachers believe they have a gift for giving;
it drives them with the same irrepressible drive
that drives others to create a work of art or a
market or a building.

—*A. Bartlett Giamatti, American educator*

Introduction

Winston Churchill said, "We make a living by what we get; we make a life by what we give." It is impossible to quantify what our best teachers have given to us. What care givers, other than our parents, help shape who we are, and who we will become, as much as our teachers do?

The Gift of Teaching honors teachers, and is meant to warmly thank them for generously sharing their knowledge. Gathered here are hundreds of quotations, ebbing and flowing like a conversation among great thinkers. There are writers and historians, educators and humorists, philosophers and scientists—each adding insight about the myriad aspects of teaching and learning. Albert Einstein and Kahlil Gibran speak passionately about the art of teaching; Judy Blume and Chinua Achebe offer insight into the child's worldview; Angela Carter and Ernest Hemingway extol the love of learning and the value of experience; while Helen Keller and Thomas Jefferson remind us to follow our hopes and dreams.

So whether you're a teacher looking for an extra ounce of inspiration to get you through the day, or a student trying to get motivated before hitting the books, or simply a lifelong learner looking for some wisdom beyond the classroom walls, it is our hope that *The Gift of Teaching* lives up to its promise to both encourage and inspire.

—Carol Kelly-Gangi and Jude Patterson
Rumson, New Jersey and
Kingston, New York, 2002

The Art of Teaching

The art of teaching is the art of assisting discovery.

—*Mark Van Doren, American poet and editor*

The whole art of teaching is only the art of awakening the natural curiosity of young minds for the purpose of satisfying it afterwards.

—*Anatole France, French writer*

I am not a teacher ... I am an awakener.

—*Robert Frost, American poet*

There is no real teacher who in practise does not believe in the existence of the soul, or in a magic that acts on it through speech.

—*Allan Bloom, American educator*

Life is amazing: and the teacher had better prepare himself to be a medium for that amazement.

—*Edward Blishen, British writer*

A teacher must believe in the value and interest of his subject as a doctor believes in health.

—*Gilbert Highet, American classicist*

Who dares to teach must never cease to learn.

—*John Colton Dana, American librarian*

9.2.03

We learn by teaching.

—*James Howell, British diplomat*

A liberal education is at the heart of a civil society, and at the heart of a liberal education is the act of teaching.

—*A. Bartlett Giamatti, American educator*

The office of the scholar is to cheer, to raise, and to guide men by showing them facts amidst appearances. He plies the slow, unhonored, and unpaid task of observation ... He is the world's eye.

—*Ralph Waldo Emerson, American poet*

No one should teach who is not a bit awed by the importance of the profession.

—*George E. Frasier*

A schoolmaster should have an atmosphere of awe, and walk wonderingly, as if he was amazed at being himself.

—*Walter Bagehot, British economist*

Gloom and solemnity are entirely out of place in even the most rigorous study of an art originally intended to make glad the heart of man.

—*Ezra Pound, American poet*

It is the supreme art of the teacher to awaken joy in creative expression and knowledge.

—*Albert Einstein, physicist*

A good teacher, like a good entertainer, first most hold his audience's attention. Then he can teach his lessons.

—*Hendrik John Clarke, American poet and editor*

Good teaching is one-fourth preparation and three-fourths theater.

—*Gail Godwin, American writer*

Use fewer examinations, fewer quizzes, and more essay assignments. You don't know anything about a subject until you can put your knowledge into some kind of expression.

—*Wayne C. Booth, American writer*

The mediocre teacher tells. The good teacher explains. The superior teacher demonstrates. The great teacher inspires.

—*William Arthur Ward, British novelist*

The most important part of teaching is to teach what it is to know.

—*Simone Weil, French philosopher*

Those who are incapable of teaching young minds to reason, pretend that it is impossible. The truth is, they are fonder of making their pupils talk well than think well; and much the greater number are better qualified to give praise to a ready memory than a sound judgment.

—*Oliver Goldsmith, British novelist*

If you are truly serious abut preparing your child for the future, don't teach him to subtract—teach him to deduct.

—*Fran Lebowitz, American journalist*

Teaching is painful, continual, and difficult work to be done by kindness, by watching and by praise, but above all by example.

—*John Ruskin, British art critic*

Have the self-command you wish to inspire ...
Teach them to hold their tongues by holding
your own. Say little; do not snarl; do not chide;
but govern by the eye. See what they need, and
that the right thing is done.

—*Ralph Waldo Emerson, American poet*

Children have never been very good at listen-
ing to their elders, but they have never failed to
imitate them.

—*James Baldwin, American writer*

Example is the school of mankind, and they
will learn at no other.

—*Edmund Burke, British politician and writer*

Teach by doing whenever you can, and only fall back upon words when doing it is out of the question.

—*Jean-Jacques Rousseau, French philosopher*

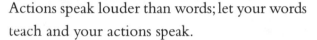

Actions speak louder than words; let your words teach and your actions speak.

—*Saint Anthony of Padua,*
Portuguese Franciscan monk

I hear and I forget.
I see and I remember.
I do and I understand.

—*Chinese proverb*

The role of the teacher [is] one of directing activity rather than actually teaching.

—*Terry Malloy, American writer*

Teaching is an instinctual art, mindful of potential, craving of realizations, a pausing, seamless process.

—*A. Bartlett Giamatti, American educator*

A teacher makes two ideas where only one grew before.

—*Elbert Hubbard, American writer*

Knowledge—like the sky—is never private property. No teacher has a right to withhold it from anyone who asks for it. Teaching is the art of sharing.

—*Abraham Joshua Heschel,*
Polish-born theologian

If you have the knowledge, let others light their candles by it.

—*Thomas Fuller, British cleric*

The true aim of everyone who aspires to be a teacher should not be to impart his own opinion, but to kindle minds.

—*Frederick William Robertson,*
British literary critic

To know how to suggest is the great art of teaching. To attain it we must be able to guess what will interest; we must learn to read the childish soul as we might a piece of music. Then, by simply changing the key, we keep up the attraction and vary the song.

—*Henri-Frédéric Amiel, Swiss poet*
and philosopher

The true teacher defends his pupils against his own personal influence. He inspires self-distrust. He guides their eyes from himself to the spirit that quickens him. He will have no disciple.

—*Amos Bronson Alcott, American*
educator and philosopher

When I transfer my knowledge, I teach. When I transfer my beliefs, I indoctrinate.

—*Arthur Danto, American essayist and educator*

The good teacher ... discovers the natural gifts of his pupils and liberates them by the stimulating influence of the inspiration that he can impart. The true leader makes his followers twice the men they were before.

—*Stephen Neill, American writer*

If [the teacher] is indeed wise he does not bid you enter the house of his wisdom, but rather leads you to the threshold of your own mind.

—*Kahlil Gibran, Lebanese-born poet*

I like to have a thing suggested rather than told in full. When every detail is given, the mind rests satisfied and the imagination loses the desire to use its own wings.

—*Thomas Bailey Aldrich, American editor*

He who wishes to teach us a truth should not tell it to us, but simply suggest it with a brief gesture, a gesture which starts an ideal trajectory in the air along which we glide until we find ourselves at the feet of the new truth.

—*José Ortega y Gasset, Spanish philosopher*

A master can tell you what he expects of you. A teacher, though, awakens your own expectations.

—*Patricia Neal, American actress*

Children should be led to make their own investigations and to draw their own inferences. They should be *told* as little as possible and induced to *discover* as much as possible. Humanity has progressed solely by self-instruction.

—*Herbert Spencer, British social philosopher*

The Master is, above all, an embodiment of Truth, and to follow the Master is to follow that Truth which is equally in ourselves.

—*N. Sri Ram, Indian writer*

There is no method of teaching that of which anyone is ignorant but by means of something already known.

—*Samuel Johnson, British writer*

Let [your scholar] know nothing because you have told him, but because he has learned it for himself. Let him not be taught science, let him discover it. If ever you substitute authority for reason, he will cease to reason; he will be a mere plaything of other people's thoughts.

—*Jean-Jacques Rousseau, French philosopher*

What matters is not what any individual thinks, but what is true. A teacher who does not equip his pupils with the rudimentary tools to discover this is substituting indoctrination for teaching.

—*Richard Stanley Peters, British educator*

I do not believe that we can put into anyone ideas which are not in him already.

—*Albert Schweitzer, German philosopher and philanthropist*

The best teacher is the one who suggests rather than dogmatizes, and inspires his listener with the wish to teach himself.

—*Edward Bulwer-Lytton, British novelist*

Partners in Learning

If a child is to keep alive his inborn sense of wonder, he needs the companionship of at least one adult who can share it, rediscovering with him the joy, excitement and mystery of the world we live in.

—*Rachel Carson, American environmentalist*

I'm not a teacher: only a fellow-traveler of whom you asked the way. I pointed ahead—ahead of myself as well as you.

—*George Bernard Shaw, Irish dramatist*

"Teachers" . . . treat students neither coercively nor instrumentally but as joint seekers of truth and of mutual actualization.

—*James MacGregor Burns, American historian*

Wherever there are beginners and experts, old and young, there is some kind of learning going on, and some sort of teaching. We are all pupils and we are all teachers.

—*Gilbert Highet, American classicist*

To teach is to learn twice over.

—*Joseph Joubert, French ethicist and essayist*

Let the teacher go into a village and take part in the crafts which are being practiced there, along with his pupils.

—*Vinoba Bhave, Indian political activist*

The teacher is no longer merely the-one-who-teaches, but one who is himself taught in dialogue with the students, who in turn while being taught also teach.

—*Paulo Freire, Brazilian educator*

You can learn many things from children. How much patience you have, for instance.

—*Franklin P. Jones, American humorist*

A young and vital child knows no limit to his own will, and it is the only reality to him. It is not that he wants at the outset to fight other wills, but that they simply do not exist for him. Like the artist, he goes forth to the work of creation, gloriously alone.

—*Jane Harrison, British classical scholar*

Nothing fortuitous happens in a child's world. There are no accidents. Everything is connected with everything else and everything can be explained by everything else ... For a young child everything that happens is a necessity.

—*John Berger, British novelist*

For truly it is to be noted, that children's plays are not sports, and should be deemed as their most serious actions.

—*Michel de Montaigne, French essayist*

Play is often talked about as if it were a relief from serious learning. But for children play is serious learning. Play is really the work of childhood.

—*Fred Rogers, American TV personality*

Why . . . do some writers talk as if care and worry were the special characteristics of adult life? It appears to me that there is more atra cura in an average schoolboy's week than in a grown man's average year.

—*C. S. Lewis, British novelist*

Children are young, but they're not naïve. And they're honest. They're not going to keep awake if the story is boring. When they get excited you can see it in their eyes.

—*Chinua Achebe, Nigerian novelist*

Oh, what a tangled web do parents weave when they think that their children are naïve.

—*Ogden Nash, American humorist*

Children are unpredictable. You never know what inconsistency they're going to catch you in next.

—*Franklin P. Jones, American humorist*

For success in training children the first condition is. . . to be as entirely and simply taken up with the child as the child himself is absorbed by his life.

—*Ellen Key, Swedish writer and feminist*

Something awful happens to a person who grows up as a creative kid and suddenly finds no creative outlet as an adult.

—*Judy Blume, American writer*

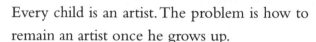

Every child is an artist. The problem is how to remain an artist once he grows up.

—*Pablo Picasso, Spanish artist*

Don't laugh at a youth for his affectations; he is only trying on one face after another to find a face of his own.

—*Logan Pearsall Smith, American essayist*

The adult works to perfect his environment, whereas the child works to perfect himself, using the environment as the means ... The child is a being in a constant state of transformation.

—*E. M. Standing, Montessori biographer*

Loving a child doesn't mean giving in to all his whims; to love him is to bring out the best in him, to teach him to love what is difficult.

—*Nadia Boulanger, French music teacher*

As the heart makes the home, the teacher makes the child.

—*Proverb*

Knowledge has outstripped character development, and the young today are given an education rather than an upbringing.

—*Ilya Ehrenburg, Russian novelist*

Mankind have been created for the sake of one another. Either instruct them, therefore, or endure them.

—*Marcus Aurelius, Roman emperor and philosopher*

To me the sole hope of human salvation lies in teaching.

—*George Bernard Shaw, Irish dramatist*

If help and salvation are to come, they can only come from the children, for the children are the makers of men.

—*Maria Montessori, Italian educator*

To rescue our children we will have to let them save us from the power we embody: we will have to trust the very difference that they forever personify.

—*June Jordan, American civil rights activist*

I consider a human soul without an education like marble in a quarry, which shows none of its inherent beauties until the skill of the polisher sketches out the colors, makes the surface shine, and discovers every ornamental cloud, spot, and vein that runs through it.

—*Joseph Addison, British essayist*

The task of education is to make the individual so firm and sure that, as a whole being, he can no longer be diverted from his path.

—*Friedrich Nietzsche, German philosopher*

He who helps a child helps humanity with an immediateness which no other help given to human creatures in any other stage of human life can possibly be given.

—*Phillips Brooks, American cleric*

Every child comes with the message that God is not yet discouraged of man.

—*Rabindranath Tagore, Indian writer*

Cherishing children is the mark of a civilized society.

> —*Joan Ganz Cooney, American children's TV producer*

It is noble to be good, and it's nobler to teach others to be good, and less trouble.

> —*Mark Twain, American humorist*

One good teacher in a lifetime may sometimes change a delinquent into a solid citizen.

> —*Philip Wylie, American writer*

'Tis education forms the common mind, Just as the twig is bent, the tree's inclined.

> —*Alexander Pope, British poet*

To educate a person in mind and not in morals is to educate a menace to society.

—*Theodore Roosevelt, American president*

Education, more than nature, is the cause of that great difference which we see in the characters of men.

—*Lord Chesterfield, British politician and writer*

Intelligence plus character—that is the goal of true education.

—*Martin Luther King Jr.,*
American civil rights leader

It is because the body is a machine that education is possible. Education is the formation of habits, a superinducing of an artificial organisation upon the natural organisation of the body.

—*Thomas Henry Huxley, British biologist*

It is just as important, perhaps more important, for the teacher to have the benefit of personal counseling when he needs it as it is for the student.

—*William Menninger, American psychiatrist*

If there is anything that we wish to change in the child, we should first examine it and see whether it is not something that could better be changed in ourselves.

—*Carl Jung, Swiss psychiatrist*

Children need models rather than critics.

—*Joseph Joubert, French ethicist and essayist*

Living up to basic ethical standards in the classroom—discipline, tolerance, honesty—is one of the most important ways children learn how to function in society at large.

—*Eloise Salholz, American journalist*

In the Classroom

It is essential to enjoy the conditions of teaching, to feel at home in a room containing twenty or thirty healthy young people, and to make our enjoyment of this group-feeling give us energy for our teaching.

— *Gilbert Highet, American classicist*

Arrange the children, sending each one to his own place, in order, trying to make them understand the idea that thus placed they look well, and that it is a good thing to be thus placed in order, that it is a good and pleasing arrangement in the room, this ordered and tranquil adjustment of theirs.

— *Maria Montessori, Italian educator*

Most learning is not the result of instruction. It is rather the result of unhampered participation in a meaningful setting.

—*Ivan Illich, American theologian*

Calming down a noisy, rebellious group of adolescents is a lot like defusing a bomb. Careful, premeditated, calm responses are crucial to success.

—*James Nehring, American educator*

When a teacher calls a boy by his entire name it means trouble.

—*Mark Twain, American humorist*

O vain futile frivolous boy. Smirking. I won't have it. I won't have it. Go find the headmaster and ask him to beat you within an inch of your life. And say please.

—*Alan Bennett, British dramatist*

The teacher should never lose his temper in the presence of the class. If a man, he may take refuge in profane soliloquies; if a woman, she may follow the example of one sweet-faced and apparently tranquil girl—go out in the yard and gnaw a post.

—*William Lyon Phelps, American educator*

One of the greatest benefits that God ever gave me is that he sent me so sharp and severe parents and so gentle a schoolmaster.

—*Lady Jane Grey, British royal*

There is no such whetstone, to sharpen a good wit and encourage a will to learning, as is praise.

—*Roger Ascham, British scholar*

[Pupils] more willingly attend to one who gives directions than to one who finds faults.

—*Quintilian, Roman rhetorician*

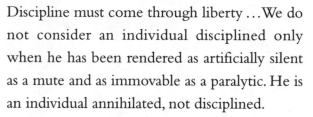

Discipline must come through liberty ... We do not consider an individual disciplined only when he has been rendered as artificially silent as a mute and as immovable as a paralytic. He is an individual annihilated, not disciplined.

—*Maria Montessori, Italian educator*

A child must feel the flush of victory and the heart-sinking of disappointment before he takes with a will to the tasks distasteful to him and resolves to dance his way through a dull routine of textbooks.

—Helen Keller, American writer and lecturer

The main value of homework lies in the experience it gives a child to work on his own.

—Haim Ginott, Israeli psychologist

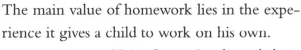

Any place that anyone can learn something useful from someone with experience is an educational institution.

—Al Capp, American cartoonist

School is where you go between when your parents can't take you and industry can't take you.

—*John Updike, American novelist*

There must be such a thing as a child with average ability, but you can't find a parent who will admit that it is his child.

—*Thomas Bailey, American educator*

True education makes for inequality; the inequality of individuality, the inequality of success, the glorious inequality of talent, of genius; for inequality, not mediocrity, individual superiority, not standardization, is the measure of the progress of the world.

—*Felix E. Schelling, American educator*

Now, if the principle of toleration were once admitted into classical education...all might in their own way arrive there.

—*Harriet Beecher Stowe, American writer*

The essence of our effort to see that every child has a chance must be to assure each an equal opportunity, not to become equal, but to become different—to realize whatever unique potential of body, mind and spirit he or she possesses.

—*John Fischer, American educator*

How do you explain school to a higher intelligence?

—*Melissa Mathison, American screenwriter*

A school is not a factory. Its raison d'être is to provide opportunity for experience.

—*J. L. Carr, British novelist*

[A school should be] a prepared environment in which the child, set free from undue adult intervention, can live its life according to the laws of its development.

—*Maria Montessori, Italian educator*

To be in the weakest camp is to be in the strongest school.

—*G. K. Chesterton, British writer*

School was an unspeakable bore and the only thing that interested me was the teacher. The rest of my studies seemed pretty worthless. Algebra and geometry were tools of the devil, devised to make life miserable for small stupid boys.

—*Groucho Marx, American comedian*

I think sleeping was my problem in school. If school had started at 4:00 in the afternoon, I'd be a college graduate today.

—*George Foreman, American professional boxer*

School is about two parts ABCs to fifty parts Where Do I Stand in the Great Pecking Order of Humankind.

—*Barbara Kingsolver, American novelist*

Twenty years of schoolin'
And they put you on the day shift.

—*Bob Dylan, American musician*

The long schooling is a way of keeping the young on ice.

—*Paul Goodman, American literary critic*

A man who has never gone to school may steal from a freight car; but if he has a university education, he may steal the whole railroad.

—*Theodore Roosevelt, American president*

College is wonderful because it takes the children away from home just as they reach the arguing stage.

—*Will Rogers, American humorist*

A Harvard education consists of what you learn at Harvard while you are not studying.

—*James Bryant Conant, American educator*

A university's essential character is that of being a center of free inquiry and criticism—a thing not to be sacrificed for anything else.

—*Richard Hofstadter, American educator*

One of the marks of the new school and the new university will be the provision of hours of withdrawal, not spent in classroom study or in sport, in the midst of its regular work day: a period of concentration and reflection, in which the work of active selection and spiritual assimilation can go on.

—*Lewis Mumford, American social critic*

The importance of these [college] years for an American cannot be overestimated. They are civilization's only chance to get to him.

—*Allan Bloom, American educator and writer*

When I give a lecture, I accept that people look at their watches, but what I do not tolerate is when they look at it and raise it to their ear to find out if it stopped.

—*Marcel Archard, french filmmaker*

A lecturer often makes you feel dumb at one end and numb at the other.

—*Evan Esar, American humorist*

If we have to have an exam at 11, let us make it one for humour, sincerity, imagination, character—and where is the examiner who could test such qualities.

—*Alexander Sutherland Neill, Scottish educator*

Examinations are formidable even to the best prepared, for the greatest fool may ask more than the wisest man can answer.

—*C. C. Colton, British cleric*

A university professor set an examination question in which he asked what is the difference between ignorance and apathy. The professor had to give an A+ to a student who answered: I don't know and I don't care.

—*Richard Pratt, American philosopher*

There is only one curriculum, no matter what the method of education: what is basic and universal in human experience and practice, the underlying structure of culture.

—*Paul Goodman, American literary critic*

Remember civics? It wasn't this bouillabaisse they call social studies today.

—*John A. Wolter, American librarian*

It is hard to convince a high school student that he will encounter a lot of problems more difficult than those of algebra and geometry.

—*Edgar Watson Howe, American editor and writer*

Math was my worst subject because I could never persuade the teacher that my answers were meant ironically.

—*Calvin Trillin, American journalist and author*

Stand firm in your refusal to remain conscious during algebra. In real life, I assure you, there is no such thing as algebra.

—*Fran Lebowitz, American journalist*

Science is for those who learn; poetry, for those who know.

—*Joseph Roux, French cleric*

Language study is a route to maturity. Indeed, in language study as in life, if a person is the same today as he was yesterday, it would be an act of mercy to pronounce him dead and to place him in a coffin, rather than in a classroom.

—*John A. Rassias, American educator*

There is a negative proof of the value of Latin: No one seems to boast of not knowing it.

—*Peter Brodie, American teacher*

Learn to write well, or not to write at all.

—*John Sheffield, British nobleman*

He that will write well in any tongue, must follow this counsel of Aristotle, to speak as the common people do, to think as wise men do; and so should every man understand him, and the judgement of wise men allow him.

—*Roger Ascham, British scholar*

Reading maketh a full man; conference a ready man; and writing an exact man.

—*Francis Bacon, British philosopher*

Books are the quietest and most constant of friends; they are the most accessible and wisest of counselors, and the most patient of teachers.

—*Charles W. Eliot, American educator*

The only books that influence us are those for which we are ready, and which have gone a little farther down our particular path than we have yet got ourselves.

—*E. M. Forster, British novelist*

The library is the temple of learning, and learning has liberated more people than all the wars in history.

—*Carl Rowan, American journalist*

Sometimes when I stand in a big library, I feel a sober, earnest delight which is hard to convey. These are not books, lumps of lifeless paper, but minds alive on the shelves.

—*Gilbert Highet, American classicist*

Read not to contradict and confute; nor to believe and take for granted; nor to find talk and discourse; but to weigh and consider.

—*Francis Bacon, British philosopher*

The love of learning, the sequestered nooks,
And all the sweet serenity of books.

—*Henry Wadsworth Longfellow, American poet*

To learn to read is to light a fire; every syllable that is spelled out is a spark.

—*Victor Hugo, French writer*

A Love of Learning

It is a glorious fever, that desire to know.

—Edward Bulwer-Lytton, British novelist

The important thing is not so much that every child should be taught, as that every child should be given the wish to learn.

—Sir John Lubbock, British naturalist

The quest for knowledge is, at bottom, the search for the answer to the question: "Where was I before I was born."

—Angela Carter, British novelist

All men by nature desire knowledge.

—Aristotle, Greek philosopher

I am always ready to learn, although I do not always like being taught.

—Winston Churchill, British statesman

If you know a thing only qualitatively, you know it no more than vaguely. If you know it quantitively—grasping some numerical measure that distinguishes it from an infinite number of other possibilities—you are beginning to know it deeply.

—Carl Sagan, American astronomer

All knowledge is ambiguous.

—J. S. Habgood, British ecclesiastic

We're drowning in information and starving for knowledge.

—*Rutherford D. Rogers, American librarian*

Knowledge is not a passion from without the mind, but an active exertion of the inward strength, vigour and power of the mind, displaying itself from within.

—*Ralph J. Cudworth, British philosopher*

If most of us are ashamed of shabby clothes and shoddy furniture, let us be more ashamed of shabby ideas and shoddy philosophies.

—*Albert Einstein, physicist*

There are no dangerous thoughts; thinking itself is dangerous.

—*Hannah Arendt, political philosopher*

If you make people think they're thinking, they'll love you: but if you really make them think, they'll hate you.

—*Don Marquis, American journalist*

I find that a great part of the information I have was acquired by looking up something and finding something else on the way.

—*Franklin Pierce Adams, American humorist*

A man should keep his little brain attic stocked with all the furniture that he is likely to use, and the rest he can put away in the lumber room of his library, where he can get it if he wants it.

—*Sir Arthur Conan Doyle, British novelist*

Knowing a lot ... is a springboard to creativity.

—*Charlie Rose, American journalist*

I know that creation is an intellectual and bodily discipline, a school of energy. I have never achieved anything in anarchy or physical slackness.

—*Albert Camus, French philosophical writer*

The invention of IQ did a great disservice to creativity in education … Individuality, personality, originality, are too precious to be meddled with by amateur psychiatrists whose patterns for a "wholesome personality" are inevitably their own.

—*Joel H. Hildebrand, American educator*

Only the curious will learn and only the resolute overcome the obstacles to learning. The quest quotient has always excited me more than the intelligence quotient.

—*Eugene S. Wilson, American educator*

Life was meant to be lived, and curiosity must be kept alive. One must never, for whatever reason, turn his back on life.

—*Eleanor Roosevelt, American diplomat*

Curiosity is one of the most permanent and certain characteristics of a vigorous intellect.

—Samuel Johnson, British lexicographer

To be wholly devoted to some intellectual exercise is to have succeeded in life.

—Robert Louis Stevenson, Scottish novelist

The function of a genius is not to give new answers, but to pose new questions which time and mediocrity can resolve.

—Hugh Trevor-Roper, British historian

A little knowledge that acts is worth infinitely more than much knowledge that is idle.

—Kahlil Gibran, Lebanese-born poet

One is not born a genius: one becomes a genius.

—*Simone de Beauvoir, French writer*

Genius is only a greater aptitude for patience.
—*Georges-Louis Leclerc, Comte de Buffon, French*
naturalist

Our observation of nature must be diligent, our reflection profound, and our experiments exact. We rarely see these three means [of acquiring knowledge] combined; and for this reason, creative geniuses are not common.

—*Denis Diderot, French philosopher*

There can be no knowledge without emotion ... To the cognition of the brain must be added the experience of the soul.

—*Arnold Bennett, British novelist*

Men have had every advantage of us in telling their own story. Education has been theirs in so much higher a degree; the pen has been in their hands.

—*Jane Austen, British novelist*

We live in a time of such rapid change and growth of knowledge that only he who is in a fundamental sense a scholar—that is, a person who continues to learn and inquire—can hope to keep pace, let alone play the role of guide.

—*Nathan M. Pusey, American educator*

The illiterate of the 21st century will not be those who cannot read and write, but those who cannot learn, unlearn, and relearn.

—*Alvin Toffler, American writer*

Anyone who stops learning is old, whether at twenty or eighty. Anyone who keeps learning stays young. The greatest thing in life is to keep your mind young.

—*Henry Ford, American automaker*

Everyone should learn to do one thing supremely well because he likes it, and one thing supremely well because he detests it.

—*B. W. M. Young, British headmaster*

I'd rather be a failure at something I enjoy than be a success at something I hate.

—*George Burns, American comedian*

[According to Muhammad], men are either learned or learning: the rest are blockheads.

—*Ralph Waldo Emerson, American poet*

There are only two kinds of people who are really fascinating—people who know absolutely everything, and people who know absolutely nothing.

—*Oscar Wilde, Irish writer*

The trouble with the world is that the stupid are cocksure and the intelligent are full of doubt.

—*Bertrand Russell, British philosopher*

Everybody is ignorant, only on different subjects.

—*Will Rogers, American humorist*

Ignorance is an evil weed, which dictators may cultivate among their dupes, but which no democracy can afford among its citizens.

—*Sir William Beveridge, British economist*

It is certain, in any case, that ignorance, allied with power, is the most ferocious enemy justice can have.

—*James Baldwin, American writer*

No amount of charters, direct primaries, or short ballots will make a democracy out of an illiterate people.

—*Walter Lippmann, American journalist*

Knowledge about life is one thing; effective occupation of a place in life, with its dynamic currents passing through your being, is another.

—*William James, American philosopher*

All experience is an arch, to build upon.

—*Henry Brooks Adams, American historian*

For the things we have to learn before we can do them, we learn by doing them.

—*Aristotle, Greek philosopher*

There are some things which cannot be learned quickly, and time, which is all we have, must be paid heavily for their acquiring. They are the very simplest things and because it takes a man's life to know them the little new that each man gets from life is very costly and the only heritage he has to leave.

—*Ernest Hemingway, American writer*

Most of the most important experiences that truly educate cannot be arranged ahead of time with any precision.

—*Harold Taylor, American educator*

Experience is a good teacher, but she sends in terrific bills.

—*Minna Antrim, American epigrammatist*

Experience is a hard teacher because she gives the test first, the lesson afterward.

—*Vernon Law, American athlete*

Experience comprises illusions lost, rather than wisdom gained.

—*Joseph Roux, French cleric*

You learn more from getting your butt kicked than from getting it kissed.

—*Tom Hanks, American actor*

The value of experience is not in seeing much, but in seeing wisely.

—*Sir William Osler, Canadian physician and educator*

We should be careful to get out of an experience only the wisdom that is in it—and stop there; lest we be like the cat that sits down on a hot stove-lid. She will never sit down on a hot stove-lid again—and that is well; but also she will never sit down on a cold one any more.

—*Mark Twain, American humorist*

You have to believe in God before you can say there are things that man was not meant to know. I don't think there's anything man wasn't meant to know. There are just some stupid things that people shouldn't do.

—*David Cronenberg, Canadian filmmaker*

If you would be a real seeker after truth, it is necessary that at least once in your life you doubt, as far as possible, all things.

—*René Descartes, French philosopher*

The first key to wisdom is assiduous and frequent questioning... For by doubting we come to inquiry, and by inquiry we arrive at truth.

—*Peter Abelard, French philosopher*

It is the province of knowledge to speak, and it is the privilege of wisdom to listen.

—*Oliver Wendell Holmes Sr., American physician*

My joy in learning is partly that it enables me to teach.

—*Seneca, Roman writer and tutor*

The Rewards of Teaching

My heart is singing for joy this morning. A miracle has happened! The light of understanding has shone upon my little pupil's mind, and, behold, all things are changed!

> —*Anne Sullivan, American educator of the deaf and blind*

The greatest sign of success for a teacher ... is to be able to say, "The children are now working as if I did not exist."

> —*Maria Montessori, Italian educator*

I'm never going to be a movie star. But then, in all probability, Liz Taylor is never going to teach first and second grade.

—*Mary J. Wilson, American teacher*

The only reason I always try to meet and know the parents better is because it helps me to forgive their children.

—*Louis Johannot, Swiss headmaster*

If you promise not to believe everything your child says happens at this school, I'll promise not to believe everything he says happens at home.

—*A British schoolmaster to his students' parents*

I see the mind of the 5-year-old as a volcano with two vents: destructiveness and creativeness.

—*Sylvia Ashton-Warner, American teacher*

When you are dealing with a child, keep all your wits about you and sit on the floor.

—*Austin O'Malley, American educator*

I have one rule—attention. They give me theirs and I give them mine.

—*Sister Evangelist R.S.M., American teacher*

I make honorable things pleasant to children.

—*A Spartan teacher*

I never reprimand a boy in the evening—darkness and a troubled mind are a poor combination.

—*Frank L. Boyden, American headmaster*

We aim to develop physique, mentality and character in our students; but because the first two are menaces without the third, the greatest of these is character.

—*Joseph Dana Allen, American headmaster*

I cannot join the space program and restart my life as an astronaut, but this opportunity to connect my abilities as an educator with my interests in history and space is a unique opportunity to fulfill my early fantasies.

—*Christa McAuliffe, American teacher*

On a good day, I view the job [of president of Yale] as directing an orchestra. On the dark days, it is more like that of a clutch—engaging the engine to effect forward motion, while taking greater friction.

—*A. Bartlett Giamatti, American educator*

I find the three major administrative problems on a campus are sex for the students, athletics for the alumni, and parking for the faculty.

—*Clark Kerr, American educational reformer*

At college age, you can tell who is best at taking tests and going to school, but you can't tell who the best people are. That worries the hell out of me.

—*Barnaby C. Keeney, American educator*

Teaching is not a lost art, but the regard for it is a lost tradition.

—*Jacques Barzun, French-born educator*

We have inadvertently designed a system in which being good at what you do as a teacher is not formally rewarded, while being poor at what you do is seldom corrected nor penalized.

—*Elliot W. Eisner, American educator*

Housework is a breeze. Cooking is a pleasant diversion. Putting up a retaining wall is a lark. But teaching is like climbing a mountain.

—*Fawn M. Brodie, American writer*

For every person who wants to teach there are approximately thirty who don't want to learn—much.

—*W. C. Sellar and R. J. Yeatman, British writers*

Schoolteachers are not fully appreciated by parents until it rains all day Saturday.

—*E. C. McKenzie, American humorist*

Genuine appreciation of other people's children is one of the rarer virtues.

—*Henry Miller, American novelist*

A teacher is the child's third parent.

—*Hyman Maxwell Berston, American educator*

We should honor our teachers more than our parents, because while our parents cause us to live, our teachers cause us to live well.

—*Philoxenus, Greek poet*

What office is there which involves more responsibility, which requires more qualifications, and which ought, therefore, to be more honourable, than that of teaching?

—*Harriet Martineau, British writer*

Everywhere, we learn only from those whom we love.

—*Johann Wolfgang Von Goethe,*
German poet and dramatist

Kids go where there is excitement. They stay where there is love.

—*Zig Ziglar, American motivational speaker*

We teachers can only help the work going on, as servants wait upon a master.

—*Maria Montessori, Italian educator*

I touch the future. I teach.

—*Christa McAuliffe, American teacher*

In a completely rational society, the best of us would aspire to be teachers and the rest of us would have to settle for something less, because passing civilization along from one generation to the next ought to be the highest honor and highest responsibility anyone could have.

—*Lee Iacocca, American corporate executive*

We shall never learn to feel and respect our real calling and destiny, unless we have taught ourselves to consider every thing as moonshine, compared with the education of the heart.

—*Sir Walter Scott, Scottish writer*

No bubble is so iridescent or floats longer than that blown by the successful teacher.

—*Sir William Osler, Canadian physician*

Successful teachers are surpassed by their pupils.

—*Anonymous*

A teacher affects eternity; he can never tell where his influence stops.

—*Henry Brooks Adams, American historian*

One looks back with appreciation to the brilliant teachers, but with gratitude to those who touched our human feelings. The curriculum is so much necessary raw material, but warmth is the vital element for the growing plant and for the soul of the child.

—*Carl Jung, Swiss psychiatrist*

A teacher's major contribution may pop out anonymously in the life of some ex-student's grandchild.

—*Wendell Berry, American poet and teacher*

When you teach your son, you teach your son's son.

—*The Talmud*

In teaching you cannot see the fruit of a day's work. It is invisible and remains so, maybe for twenty years.

—*Jacques Barzun, French-born educator*

Wisdom and Inspiration

It is never too late to learn.

—English proverb

Become the lesson you would teach; be what you would have others become.

—Anonymous

You cannot put an old head on young shoulders.

—English proverb

Ask a silly question and you get a silly answer.

—English proverb

There is no royal road to learning.

—English proverb

Learning is like rowing upstream; not to advance is to drop back.

—Chinese proverb

The difficult we do immediately; the impossible takes a little longer.

—Slogan of U.S. Armed Forces

An ounce of practice is worth a pound of precept.

—English proverb

When the student is ready, the teacher arrives; when the teacher is ready, the student arrives.

—*Anonymous*

Teachers open the door, but you must enter by yourself.

—*Chinese proverb*

Education is not preparation for life; education is life itself.

—*John Dewey, American educator*

Education is not the filling of a pail, but the lighting of a fire.

—*William Butler Yeats, Irish poet*

To me education is a leading out of what is already there in the pupil's soul.

—*Muriel Spark, British novelist*

Education is a private matter between the person and the world of knowledge and experience, and has little to do with school or college.

—*Lillian Smith, American novelist*

A single conversation across the table with a wise man is better than ten years' mere study of books.

—*Henry Wadsworth Longfellow, American poet*

The world of knowledge takes a crazy turn
When teachers themselves are taught to learn.

—*Bertolt Brecht, German dramatist*

The ideal condition
Would be, I admit, that men should be right by
instinct;
But since we are all likely to go astray,
The reasonable thing is to learn from those
who can teach.

—*Sophocles, Greek dramatist*

But where's the man who counsel can bestow,
Still pleas'd to teach, and yet not proud to
know?

—*Alexander Pope, British poet*

The vanity of teaching often tempteth a man to forget he is a blockhead.

—*George Savile, Lord Halifax, British statesman*

To know yet to think that one does not know is best;
Not to know yet to think that one knows will lead to difficulty.

—*Lao-tzu, Chinese philosopher*

Knowledge is proud that he has learned so much; Wisdom is humble that he knows no more.

—*William Cowper, British poet*

The world's great men have not commonly been great scholars, nor its great scholars great men.

—*Oliver Wendell Holmes Sr.,*
American physician and writer

And let a scholar all Earth's volumes carry,
He will be but a walking dictionary.

—*George Chapman, British translator*
of classic literature

The ignorant are a reservoir of daring.

—*Eric Hoffer, American philosopher*

Let him that would move the world, first move himself.

—*Socrates, Greek philosopher*

γνωθι σεαυτον
Know thyself.

—*Inscription on the temple of Apollo at Delphi*

The world is one great university. From the cradle to the grave we are always in God's great kindergarten—where everything is trying to teach its lesson.

—*O. S. Marden, American motivational writer*

In a time of drastic change it is the learners who inherit the future. The learned usually find themselves equipped to live in a world that no longer exists.

—*Eric Hoffer, American philosopher*

Nurture your mind with great thoughts. To believe in the heroic makes heroes.

—*Benjamin Disraeli, British statesman*

To know the thoughts and deeds that have marked man's progress is to feel the great heart-throbs of humanity through the centuries; and if one does not feel in these pulsations a heavenward striving, one must indeed be deaf to the harmonies of life.

—*Helen Keller, American deaf-blind writer*

I like the dreams of the future better than the history of the past.

—*Thomas Jefferson, American president*

The future belongs to those who believe in the beauty of their dreams.

—*Eleanor Roosevelt, American diplomat*

Reverie is not a mind vacuum. It is rather the gift of an hour which knows the plenitude of the soul.

—*Gaston Bachelard, French philosopher*

The imagination should be allowed a certain amount of time to browse around.

—*Thomas Merton, American Trappist monk*

The indefatigable pursuit of an unattainable perfection—even though nothing more than the pounding of an old piano—is what alone gives a meaning to our life on this unavailing star.

—*Logan Pearsall Smith, American essayist*

To be surprised, to wonder, is to begin to understand.

—*José Ortega y Gasset, Spanish philosopher*

All rising to a great place is by a winding stair.

—*Francis Bacon, British philosopher*

And all your future lies beneath your hat.

—*John Oldham, British poet*

Inspiration cannot be willed, although it can be wooed.

—*Anthony Storr, British psychiatrist*

Many times I have found that my best ideas have come when I thought I could not work for another minute and when I literally had to drive myself to finish the task before a deadline.

—*Richard M. Nixon, American president*

All my best thoughts were stolen by the ancients.

—*Ralph Waldo Emerson, American poet*

New ideas come into this world somewhat like falling meteors, with a flash and an explosion.

—*Henry David Thoreau, American naturalist*

A man gazing on the stars is proverbially at the mercy of the puddles in the road.

—*Alexander Smith, Scottish poet*

Don't aim for success if you want it; just do what you love and believe in, and it will come naturally.

—*David Frost, British journalist*

Failure is instructive. The person who really thinks learns quite as much from his failures as from his successes.

—*John Dewey, American educator*

Failure is the condiment that gives success its flavor.

—*Truman Capote, American writer*

An idealist is one who, on noticing that a rose smells better than a cabbage, concludes that it will also make better soup.

—*H. L. Mencken, American journalist*

I am an idealist. I don't know where I'm going, but I'm on my way.

—*Carl Sandburg, American poet*

A glimpse is not a vision. But to a man on a mountain road by night, a glimpse of the next three feet of road may matter more than a vision of the horizon.

—*C. S. Lewis, British novelist*

We shall not cease from exploration
And the end of all our exploring
Will be to arrive where we started
And know the place for the first time.

—*T. S. Eliot, American poet*

There are three ingredients in the good life: learning, earning, and yearning.

—*Christopher Morley, American writer and editor*

We make a living by what we get; we make a life by what we give.

—*Winston Churchill, British statesman*

The sage does not hoard.
Having bestowed all he has on others, he has yet more;
Having given all he has to others, he is richer still.

—*Lao-tzu, Chinese philosopher*

Behold, I do not give lectures or a little charity,
When I give I give myself.

—*Walt Whitman, American poet*